The Best
Thing in Life
Is a Friend

Other Bestselling Books by Blue Mountain Press

Books by Susan Polis Schutz:
To My Daughter, with Love, on the Important Things in Life
To My Son with Love
Love, Love, Love

For You, Just Because You're Very Special to Me
by Collin McCarty

100 Things to Always Remember... and One Thing to Never Forget
by Alin Austin

Anthologies:
42 Gifts I'd Like to Give to You
A Sister Is a Very Special Friend
Be Proud of All You've Achieved
The Best Thing in Life Is a Friend
Creeds to Live By, Dreams to Follow
Don't Ever Give Up Your Dreams
For a Special Teenager
For You, My Daughter
I Keep Falling in Love with You
I Want Our Love to Last Forever
Life Can Be Hard Sometimes... but It's Going to Be Okay
Marriage Is a Promise of Love
Mother, I Love You
Mother, Thank You for All Your Love
Mottos to Live By
Reach Out for Your Dreams
Take Each Day One Step at a Time
There Is Greatness Within You, My Son
Thoughts of Love
True Friends Always Remain in Each Other's Heart

Blue Mountain Press®

Boulder, Colorado

The Best
Thing in Life
Is a Friend

A collection of poems
Edited by Susan Polis Schutz

Blue Mountain Press ™

Boulder, Colorado

Library of Congress Catalog Card Number: 86-73019
ISBN: 0-88396-249-7

The following works have previously appeared in Blue Mountain Arts publications:

"A friend is," by Susan Polis Schutz. Copyright © Stephen Schutz and Susan Polis Schutz, 1980. "Some people," by Susan Polis Schutz. Copyright © Stephen Schutz and Susan Polis Schutz, 1986. "Thank You for Your Friendship," "When We Can't Be Together," and "Thank You for Being My Real Friend for Life," by Susan Polis Schutz. Copyright © Stephen Schutz and Susan Polis Schutz, 1987. "Do you know why" and "Friend . . . ," by Collin McCarty. Copyright © Blue Mountain Arts, Inc., 1985. "Deep in everyone's heart," by Paula J. Tenney; and "As Friends, We Understand Each Other," "Good Friends," "My Dear Friend," and "No Matter What," by Collin McCarty. Copyright © Blue Mountain Arts, Inc., 1986. "The Best Thing in Life Is a Friend," by Maria Elena Najera; "My Friend," by Lenore Turkeltaub; "What Is a Friend," and "I Want Us to Always Be Friends," by Collin McCarty; and "It Means So Much to Have You as a Friend," by Carey Martin. Copyright © Blue Mountain Arts, Inc., 1987.

Thanks to the Blue Mountain Arts creative staff.

ACKNOWLEDGMENTS appear on page 62.

Manufactured in the United States of America
First printing: February, 1987

Blue Mountain Press INC.

P.O. Box 4549, Boulder, Colorado 80306

CONTENTS

What Is a Friend?

A friend is one of the nicest things you can have, and one of the best things you can be. A friend is a living treasure, and if you have one, you have one of the most valuable gifts in life.

A friend is the one who will always be beside you, through all the laughter, and through each and every tear. A friend is the one thing you can

always rely on; the someone you can always
open up to; the one wonderful person who
always believes in you in a way that no one else
seems to.
A friend is a sanctuary.
A friend is a smile.

A friend is a hand that is always holding yours, no
matter where you are, no matter how close or far
apart you may be. A friend is someone who is
always there and will always — always — care.
A friend is a feeling of forever in the heart.

A friend is the one door that is always open. A
friend is the one to whom you can give your key.
A friend is one of the nicest things you can have,
and one of the best things
you can be.

— Collin McCarty

When We Can't Be Together, I Really Miss You, My Friend

I have other friends
whom I talk to
but it's not
the same
You have such
a deep understanding
of who I am
I hardly have to
speak any words
and you know just
what I am saying

I really miss you
and I want to be sure
    that you know
that no matter where I go
whom I meet
or what I do
I'll never find
as deep a friendship
with anyone as I
have with you

— Susan Polis Schutz

As Friends, We Understand Each Other

As friends,
we share so much more
than other people may ever realize . . .
We share a closeness
that is very precious
and a friendship that is very lasting.
We know we don't have to be afraid
of opening up to one another,
of trusting each other completely,
of appreciating every moment of time
    we spend in one another's company.
I'm not afraid to let you see me cry,
    and you're the one person I want to be
    with when I want to feel crazy.
Through it all, I know you understand,
    in the same way that
        I understand you.

There are other people whom I dearly love
and care about in this world,
but there is no one else quite like you.

Every time I look back,
   our friendship has been
      one of the best parts of the yesterdays.

And every time I look ahead,
   I see our friendship
as the one thing I can always count on
   to get me through tomorrow.

— Collin McCarty

Deep in everyone's heart,
there is a special corner
saved only for a very special person.
To me, you are that person.
You give me great happiness . . .
a happiness I will never take for granted,
because I feel it only when I am with you.
You bring me joy;
you cause me to wonder;
you bring me laughter.
And in your own special way,
just through the simplicity of being you,
you enrich my life
and fill my heart with peace.

For all of this, I thank you
and tell you that I am so very glad
that the special corner
   in my heart
      was meant just for you.

— Paula J. Tenney

You're the Best Friend
a Person Could Ever Have

You're in my heart and soul,
the inspiration of many of my dreams,
the very best friend a person
    could ever have.
The many dreams
    and moments we have spent
    together will never be forgotten,
times of pain, as well as happy times.
We shared laughter and love,
and you let me give you a few of
    my own tears.
Each new day with you seems brighter,
and each new moment
    seems more precious
    than the one before.
I will love you always,
    my friend.

— Claudia Kim

Do you know why
you're so special to me?
I think it's because
you're the only one
who ever took the time
and cared enough to know
what was going on inside of me.

I don't give of myself very much,
I know, but when I do,
I do it with love directed towards
the ones I know I can trust,
and who know they can trust me.
I don't know why it's so hard
   to open up to another, but it is.

And when you lay your innermost
    feelings on the line, you need to know
    that the person on the other side
    is really a friend.
You are such a precious friend to me.
Without you, I'm not really sure
    what I would do; I only know that
        I reached out to the right person . . .
        when I reached out to you.

— Collin McCarty

It Means So Much
to Have You as a Friend

You know me like no other
person ever will.
You know the story of my life,
for it is written on many of
   the same pages as yours.
You know my faults
   and weaknesses,
      my insecurities and my doubts,
         and still . . . you like me
         anyway.

You're good to me.
And you're good for me.
You're the only person who

I know for certain would be there
   trying to hold my spirits up,
if my whole world
   came crashing down.

I can't tell you
how much it means
to have you in my life.
   All I can say
      . . . is that I can't imagine
         being here without you.

   You're wonderful.
   You really are.

— Carey Martin

Some people will be your friend
because of whom you know
Some people will be your friend
because of your position
Some people will be your friend
because of the way you look
Some people will be your friend
because of your possessions
But the only real friends
are the people who will be your friends
because they like you for how you are inside
Thank you for being
one of the very few people in my life
who is a real friend

— Susan Polis Schutz

Friendship
is more than a collection
of moments;
it transcends time and distances.

Friendship anticipates needs;
it shares without hesitation.

It says, "I accept you for what you are,"
and understands your failings.

Friendship supports and nurtures,
without any need for recognition.

It belongs both to quiet moments
and to troubled times.

Friendship is love for all seasons.

— Jessica Jordan

There aren't many things
that last forever anymore.
People pass through each other's lives,
plans are mislaid,
and memories fade.

But I do want, very much,
to have something forever —
a sense of caring,
a sense of trust,
and a smile when life seems
to have hit the very bottom.

I want
a forever friendship,
and I think
I have found one with you.

— Beth Lynne Ellis

My Friend . . .

Together we have developed a friendship
based on honesty, loyalty, devotion,
respect, and love.

We have shared our time, our souls,
and our intimate thoughts,
until our shadows hugged, joined, blended,
and then moved as one.

Silently, we have felt each other's needs
and wants,
and wiped away each other's tears,
always with understanding and love.

We have accepted and encouraged one another,
respected each other's abilities,
and delighted in the other's
accomplishments.

Ours is a friendship without frills
    and garnishes,
one where we can relax and be ourselves
    without masks or roles to play.

It is a friendship that will continue
    to grow;
it is a constant source of comfort
            and joy in my life.

— Lenore Turkeltaub

That's What Friends Are For

I never thought I'd feel this way,
And as far as I'm concerned,
I'm glad I got the chance to say
That I do believe I love you.

And if I should ever go away,
Well then close your eyes and try
To feel the way we do today.
And if you can remember,
Keep smiling, keep shining,
Knowing you can always count on me,
    for sure,
That's what friends are for.
For good times, and bad times,
I'll be on your side forevermore.
That's what friends are for.

You came and opened me,
And now there's so much more I see.
And so by the way, I thank you.

And then, for the times when we're apart,
Close your eyes and know
The words are coming from my heart.
And then if you can remember,
Keep smiling, keep shining,
Knowing you can always count on me,
    for sure,
That's what friends are for.
In good times, and bad times,
I'll be on your side forevermore.
That's what friends are for.

               — Carole Bayer Sager and
                 Burt Bacharach

No Matter What,
We'll Always Be Friends

We've been through
a lot together, you and I.
And beyond the happiness
   and the tears that
      have been shared
comes something else . . .

It's a connection that
will always be there between us.
No matter where we go
   or how much time passes,
you and I will always,
   in a very special way,
      remain together in spirit.

And that knowledge
is cherished by me
as the one thing that must never change.
In a world of constant transition,
    I pray that what we feel
        towards one another
            will always stay the same.

— Collin McCarty

A friend is
someone who is concerned
with everything you do

A friend is
someone to call upon
during good and bad times

A friend is
someone who understands
whatever you do

A friend is
someone who tells you
the truth about yourself

A friend is
someone who knows
what you are going through
at all times

A friend is
someone who does not
compete with you

A friend is
someone who is genuinely happy
for you when things go well

A friend is
someone who tries to
cheer you up when
things don't go well

A friend is
an extension of yourself
without which
you are not complete

Thank you for being my friend

— Susan Polis Schutz

Your Friendship
Is the Treasure in My Life

There are treasures in one's life
   that cannot be seen,
cannot be touched,
   are impossible to measure
or estimate their value . . .
They cannot be bought,
   yet are given for free.
These precious gifts
   have been given to me
and have made a difference in my life
   through the friend I've found in you.

Understanding —
   of all our different ways.
Honesty —
   about what you think and feel.
Laughter —
   at the times we've shared.
Patience —
   with my changing moods.
Your friendship
   is among the treasures of my life —
growing as we grow,
   changing for the better,
yet remaining a steady part of my days.

— Kathi Zack

The Art of Friendship

Friendship is the art of forgetting oneself
totally, all selfish needs and wants, and
getting to know the person and character of
one another.
It's learning to accept a person not for what
they are on the outside, but for what they
reveal to you from the inside. It's
strengthening oneself with the qualities
found in a friend and the experiences
shared with each other.

It's learning and growing to care for a person in such a way that you hurt when they hurt, and you are able to feel their joy when it comes to them.

Friendship means being there to give to one another without any thought of taking, being there to support another when they are weak, or giving them your smile when they have lost their own.

Friendship is the blending of two unique souls to form a complete spirit with a common bond of love and caring.

The art of friendship, in its most basic form, is love that cares.

— Vicki McClelland Jeter

My Dear Friend

I care about you
a lot more than
I've ever told you before.
You're one of the
   closest friends I've got . . .
and I want you to know
that for all we've been through,
for all the sharing,
the encouragement,
the serious and the silly times,
and the just-being-together times,
I've come to really appreciate you.

Whenever I look at your
    smiling face,
I see a very special friend
who makes my world
    a better place to be.

Thanks . . . for sharing
        your friendship with me.

— Collin McCarty

I'm Glad I Became
Friends with You

Certain times come in your life when you notice just how much someone really means to you — simply because they have taken the time for you, to live, love, and smile with you, and hurt when you hurt.

Becoming friends with you — always having the freedom to tell you anything while feeling complete trust and comfort, knowing it is safe inside this circle we've built together — this is what makes our friendship the very best.

We have had our bad moments in which neither of us understood what the other meant, but somehow we seemed to find our way back to each other, always forgiving each other and gaining a greater respect for each other's views.

I have gathered such great memories of us, and I believe we have come so far together in this lifetime, through good and bad times, each of us making sacrifices along the way to keep our friendship going strong and forever alive.

As life continues on, I hope that you have many beautiful days ahead and that this friendship we share will grow richer and stronger with each passing moment.

— Kathleen King Richardson

I Want Us to Always Be Friends

You're such a good friend.
Sometimes I think that
the whole world could
cave in around me, but
I know that if I still had you
for my friend, everything
would be all right.

I don't want anything
to ever go wrong
with us.

There are things in the world
that I could stand to lose. . .
but if I ever lost you
as a friend,
I would lose something
invaluable . . . that could
        never be replaced.

You're an important part
    of my life,
        and you're my dearest friend.
I want us to always stay
    as close as we are today.

— Collin McCarty

We Are Such Good Friends

We both have others in our lives
whom we care so much about,
but deep in our hearts,
there's a wonderful feeling
I have for you,
and you for me.
We can talk or argue,
we can rejoice or complain,
and we both seem to understand.
In so many ways we're the same,
and yet so different.
We come from our worlds
so far apart, yet we've learned
to trust and care a lot.
Our relationship
is so very unique;

no one could ever have
    one just like it.
For the time we spend together,
we always seem to bring our two worlds
    together.
No distance, no time,
can ever lessen my feelings for you.
No person,
no place,
can ever hold the part of my heart
that only you can have.
We are such good friends,
in so many ways best friends,
for yesterday, today,
and every tomorrow.

— Shirley Oneschuk

Thank You for Your Friendship

All the time
I think how much
I'd like to thank you
for our friendship
but the right time
never seems to occur
So, please
know that I

always feel these thoughts
even though I don't say them
I am extremely proud
to call you my friend
Our friendship is
such an important part
of my life and
I am deeply grateful to you
for sharing yourself
with me

— Susan Polis Schutz

Our Friendship Is Magic

Friendship is
   a magic thing,
able to bring a smile
   from a memory;
able to share a part
   of another's life.
It doesn't matter
   how large a part;
what matters is the feeling
   of warmth it produces:
the sunshine added to the day
because of a smile freely given;
a kind thought sincerely sent.

These things are just small parts
    of the magic of friendship.
Friendship has no barriers;
only a choice to share a part
    of another's life,
however briefly,
and to let another share
    a part of your life.
I'm glad to share the magic
    of friendship
with you.

— Char Weisel

We Share a
Special Bond of Friendship

Dearest friend,
we've shared so much of our lives.
We've talked about dreams
and goals we've set.
We've shared pain
and caused one another pain,
yet a bond still remains.
It's tucked deep within our hearts.
It shares the longings,
the deeds, of our past,
and our hopes for the future.

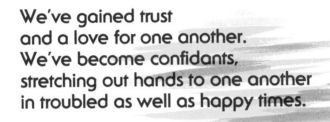

We've gained trust
and a love for one another.
We've become confidants,
stretching out hands to one another
in troubled as well as happy times.

I pray that life will continue
to strengthen the bond
that the two of us share.

— Sherrie Householder

Our Friendship Is One
That Will Live Forever

In order to appreciate
what a true friend is,
we must be willing
to allow them freedom
to grow, to expand their horizons,
and to give others
the privilege of knowing them.
By trusting them enough
to know that they care
even when they're not present,
we allow a true friend unrestricted
freedom and the chance
to be themselves.
The assurance in their friendship
comes from knowing that they
have the capacity to love
beyond all measure
and still have love left over.
They do not expect one friend
to be like another.

By knowing someone as a true friend,
we have experienced
the dearest treasure — one which will
never pass away from us,
for it is ours forever.
It is a love that cannot be restrained,
but must be allowed to grow.
We must be willing
to trust and take chances.
We must allow a true friend
to be everything that they can be;
we perhaps may not always
    understand it,
but we can always accept it.
A friendship that can accept
    and still love
is a true friendship
    that will live forever.

— Bethanie Jean Brevik

Friend . . .

One of the most special
places in my heart will always be
   saved for you.
You . . .
  the one person I can always talk to;
  the one person who understands.
You . . .
  for making me laugh in the rain;
  for helping me shoulder my troubles.
You . . .
  for loving me in spite of myself,
  and always putting me
   back on my feet again.

You . . .
    for giving me someone to believe in;
    someone who lets me know that
    there really is goodness
       and kindness
          and laughter and love
            in the world.
You . . .
    for being one of the best
    parts of my life, and proving it
        over and over again.
You . . .
    for being so worthy of my love,
      for being
        my friend.

                    — Collin McCarty

What Makes a Person a Friend?

It's the ability
  to love and care and understand
    like no one else.
It's the ability
  to make a person smile when they can't,
  to bring them up when they're down.
It's the ability
  to see through all the superficial
    smiles and know that deep inside
    the real smiles are far away,
  to make even the worst things seem
    not quite so bad,
  and the best things even better.

It's the ability
   to just look into another's eyes
   and give that person a sense of love
     that they always seem
         to need.
It's the ability
   to be trusted with a person's secrets,
     the secrets kept from everyone else.
It's the ability
   to be loved and admired by everyone
   who knows them.
It's the ability
   to be the kind of person
     that I have found in you, my friend.

— Kimberly Carney

Thank You for Being
My Real Friend for Life

It is easy to find a friend
when things are going well
and everyone can have fun together

It is easy to find a friend
when exciting things are happening
and everyone can look forward
   to them together

It is easy to find a friend
when the environment is attractive
and everyone can be happy together

But the friend that we find
who will be with us
when we are having problems
and our lives are confused
is a hard friend to find

Thank you for being
one of those rare people
who is a
real friend
for life

— Susan Polis Schutz

The Friend I Have in You

I have shared with you
the sadness in my life;
I have shared with you
   the joy.

Your listening helps me
to hear my own thoughts,
your insight helps me
to understand my problems,
and your patience helps me
   to accept my faults.

You know when I need
your advice,
and you sense when I
simply need you
    to be there.

Everything I could ever
want in a friend
I have . . .
    in you.

                — Paula Finn

Good Friends

We share something special.
We really care about
    each other's well-being.
We're good at making each other laugh.
We see so many things
    in the same ways.
I think that our hearts know
    and share cherished feelings
        . . . even if they are never spoken.

There are so many things about us
that give me reasons to feel glad.
We have a wonderful understanding.
We have a sincere appreciation.
We have a special
togetherness.

We have one of the best friendships
that I have ever known,
and that I ever hope to have.

— Collin McCarty

The Best Thing in Life Is a Friend

One of the best things about life is friends. You find them wherever you go.

Friends are essential because they help bring out the best in you. When they see your worst, they still care. They just accept.

Friends are the stars in your happy memories. In your sad memories, they are the shoulders you leaned on and the hearts that listened. They just care.

Friends help you in your times of need. When things are going smoothly, they are content to be your friend. They just know.

Friends help create all your fun times, always there to spread laughter and joy. When you need tears, friends provide these, too. They just understand.

You, my friend, are all of these. And most of all, when you need it, remember friends just love, as I do you.

— Maria Elena Najera

ACKNOWLEDGMENTS

We gratefully acknowledge the permission granted by the following authors and publishers to reprint poems and excerpts from their publications.

Kimberly Carney for "What Makes a Person a Friend," by Kimberly Carney. Copyright © Kimberly Carney, 1987. All rights reserved. Reprinted by permission.

Bethanie Jean Brevik for "Our Friendship Is One That Will Live Forever," by Bethanie Jean Brevik. Copyright © Bethanie Jean Brevik, 1987. All rights reserved. Reprinted by permission.

Sherrie Householder for "We Share a Special Bond of Friendship," by Sherrie Householder. Copyright © Sherrie Householder, 1987. All rights reserved. Reprinted by permission.

Shirley Oneschuk for "We Are Such Good Friends," by Shirley Oneschuk. Copyright © Shirley Oneschuk, 1987. All rights reserved. Reprinted by permission.

Kathleen King Richardson for "I'm Glad I Became Friends with You," by Kathleen King Richardson. Copyright © Kathleen King Richardson, 1987. All rights reserved. Reprinted by permission.

Vicki McClelland Jeter for "The Art of Friendship," by Vicki McClelland Jeter. Copyright © Vicki McClelland Jeter, 1987. All rights reserved. Reprinted by permission.

Kathi Zack for "Your Friendship Is the Treasure in My Life," by Kathi Zack. Copyright © Kathi Zack, 1987. All rights reserved. Reprinted by permission.

Jessica Jordan for "Friendship," by Jessica Jordan. Copyright © Jessica Jordan, 1987. All rights reserved. Reprinted by permission.

Beth Lynne Ellis for "There aren't many things," by Beth Lynne Ellis. Copyright © Beth Lynne Ellis, 1987. All rights reserved. Reprinted by permission.

Char Weisel for "Our Friendship Is Magic," by Char Weisel. Copyright © Char Weisel, 1987. All rights reserved. Reprinted by permission.

Paula Finn for "The Friend I Have in You," by Paula Finn. Copyright © Paula Finn, 1986. All rights reserved. Reprinted by permission.

Claudia Kim for "You're the Best Friend a Person Could Ever Have," by Claudia Kim. Copyright © Claudia Kim, 1987. All rights reserved. Reprinted by permission.

Warner Bros. Music for "That's What Friends Are For," by Carole Bayer Sager and Burt Bacharach. Copyright © 1982, 1985 WB Music Corp., New Hidden Valley Music, Warner-Tamerlane Publishing Corp. & Carole Bayer Sager Music. All rights reserved. Used by permission.

A careful effort has been made to trace the ownership of poems used in this anthology in order to obtain permission to reprint copyrighted materials and to give proper credit to the copyright owners.

If any error or omission has occurred, it is completely inadvertent, and we would like to make corrections in future editions provided that written notification is made to the publisher: BLUE MOUNTAIN PRESS, INC., P.O. Box 4549, Boulder, Colorado 80306.